ANCIENT EGYPT

Miranda Smith

KINGFISHER
NEW YORK

KINGFISHER
LONDON & NEW YORK

Copyright © Kingfisher 2010
Published in the United States by Kingfisher,
175 Fifth Ave., New York, NY 10010
Kingfisher is an imprint of Macmillan Children's Books, London.
All rights reserved.

Consultant: Margaret Maitland

Illustrations by Roger Stuart, Steve Weston, Peter Bull Art Studio

Created for Kingfisher by White-Thomson Publishing Ltd.
www.wtpub.co.uk

Distributed in the U.S. by Macmillan, 175 Fifth Ave., New York, NY 10010
Distributed in Canada by H.B. Fenn and Company Ltd., 34 Nixon Road,
Bolton, Ontario L7E 1W2

Library of Congress Cataloging-in-Publication data has been applied for.

ISBN: 978-0-7534-6429-8

Kingfisher books are available for special promotions and premiums. For details contact:
Special Markets Department, Macmillan, 175 Fifth Ave., New York, NY 10010.

For more information, please visit www.kingfisherbooks.com

Printed in China
1 3 5 7 9 8 6 4 2
1TR/0610/WKT/UG(UG)/140GSM/C

Note to readers: The website addresses listed in this book are correct at the time of publishing.
However, due to the ever-changing nature of the Internet, website addresses and content can change.
Websites can contain links that are unsuitable for children. The publisher cannot be held responsible for
changes in website addresses or content or for information obtained through third-party websites.
We strongly advise that Internet searches be supervised by an adult.

The Publisher would like to thank the following for permission to reproduce their material. Every care has been taken to trace copyright holders. However, if there has been unintentional omissions or failure to trace copyright holders, we apologize and will, if informed, endeavor to make corrections in any future edition. (t = top, b = bottom, c = center, r = right, l = left):

Front cover (mask) Getty/Digital Vision; tl Shutterstock/Mytro Korolov; tr Shutterstock/sculpies; c Shutterstock/Pavle Marjanovic; bl Getty/Bridgeman Art Library; br Getty/Bridgeman Art Library; back cover l Art Archive/Egyptian Museum Turin/Dagli Orti; r Art Archive/Staatliche Sammlung Aegyptischer Kunst, Munich/Dagli Orti; and pages 4bl Shutterstock/José Ignacio Soto; 5tr AKG/Erich Lessing; 5bl Alamy/Tor Eigeland; 5bc Photolibrary/S. Tauqueur; 7tr Bridgeman Art Library/Giraudon; 6–7b AKG/Francois Guenet; 8tr Shutterstock/BOSKO; 8 British Museum (EA 9999); 9 British Museum Harris Papyrus (EA 9999 [same]) 8–9 background Shutterstock/Maugli; 9tl Art Archive/Dagli Orti; 9tr Art Archive/Musée du Louvre/Dagli Orti; 10br Art Archive/Dagli Orti; 11tr Shutterstock/Maugli; 11bc Bridgeman Art Library/Musée du Louvre; 11br British Museum (EA 59334); 12–13 British Museum (EA 37977); 12br British Museum; 13bl British Museum (GR 1888); 13br British Museum (EA 1242); 14l British Museum (EA 15671); 14r British Museum; 15 British Museum (GR 1894, 1101.269); 17t British Museum (EA 6046 & others); 17 British Museum (EA 41187); 17 University College London, Petrie Museum of Egyptian Archaeology (UC63042); 18–19 Corbis/Yann Arthus-Bertrand; 18cr AKG/Boston Museum of Fine Arts; 19tc Art Archive/Egyptian Museum, Cairo/Dagli Orti; 19cl AKG/Feuardet Collection; 19cr Shutterstock/Vladimir Wrangel; 19bc British Museum (EA 63800); 19br Shutterstock/José Antonio Sanchez; 21bl British Museum (EA 10221); 21tr British Museum; 21br Reuters/STR New; 22tr Corbis/Stephen Vidler; 22c Art Archive/Dagli Orti; 22cr British Museum (EA 9565 &others); 24br Art Archive/Eygptian Museum/Kharbine-Tapabor/Boistesselin; 25c Photolibrary/Musée du Louvre; 25bc British Museum (EA 41548); 25br Art Archive/Musée du Louvre/Dagli Orti; 26tr Art Archive/Musée du Louvre/Dagli Orti; 27tr Art Archive/Ragab Papyrus Institute, Cairo/Dagli Orti; 28–29 Corbis/José Fuste Raga; 28tr Werner Forman Archive (WFA); 28bl AKG/Bildarchiv Steffens; 29tc Shutterstock/ligio; 29br Shutterstock/David Peta; 30tr Art Archive/Dagli Orti; 30br WFA/British Museum; 31tc WFA/British Museum; 31cr Art Archive/Dagli Orti ; 31br WFA/British Museum; 32–33 Art Archive/Egyptian Museum, Cairo/Dagli Orti; 32br AKG/Egyptian Museum, Berlin; 33tr British Museum; 33br Art Archive/Egyptian Museum, Cairo/Dagli Orti; 34bl AKG/Field Museum of Natural History, Chicago; 34–35 Art Archive/Egyptian Museum, Cairo/Dagli Orti; 35t AKG/James Morris; 35tr Shutterstock/Mirek Hejnicki; 35cr Shutterstock/Vladimir Korostychevsky; 35bc AKG/Museo Eqizio, Turin; 35br Shutterstock/Vladimir Wrangel; 36tr Shutterstock/José Ignacio Soto; 36br Art Archive/Egyptian Museum, Cairo/Dagli Orti; 37tr Shutterstock/Kletr; 37cr Shutterstock/Eric Isselee; 37c AKG/Erich Lessing; 38tl Shutterstock/ Mirek Hejnicki; 39tr Getty/Business Wire; 39cr Corbis/Hulton; 39br AKG/James Morris; 40–41 Altair 4 Multimedia Srl; 40bl Art Archive/Dagli Orti; 40tr Shutterstock/Tat Mun Lui; 41br Art Archive/Musée du Louvre/Dagli Orti; 42l Art Archive/Staatliche Glypothek, Munich/Dagli Orti; 42br British Museum (EA 1694); 43 Altair 4 Multimedia Srl; 43cr Art Archive/Egyptian Museum, Turin/Dagli Orti; 43br Art Archive/Jan Vinchon Numismatist, Paris/Dagli Orti; 48tl Shutterstock/José Ignacio Soto; 48tr Shutterstock/Baloncici; 48cl Shutterstock/Ragnarok; 48c British Museum; 48cr Shutterstock/BOSKO; 48bl Shutterstock/Adrian Lindley

CONTENTS

The black border shows the boundaries of modern-day Egypt. The highlighted section is the area of ancient Egypt shown on these two pages.

Red Sea

Mediterranean Sea

Gulf of Suez

Voyage in time

A journey down the Nile River is a journey through history. The rulers of Egypt were known as the Lords of the Two Lands. Upper Egypt was the Nile valley in the south. Lower Egypt was in the north, mainly the area of the delta. Capital cities moved to various places on the Nile as the leaders of different families became pharaohs.

"The Nile, forever new and old,
Among the living and the dead,
Its mighty, mystic stream has rolled."

Henry Wadsworth Longfellow
from The Golden Legend

LOWER EGYPT

In the north, the river separates into different branches, creating the triangular marshlands of the delta.

NILE DELTA

Egypt's most famous pyramids were built on the Giza plateau, just south of the delta.

• ALEXANDRIA

GIZA •

• SAQQARA

• MEMPHIS

• AKHETATON (AMARNA)

NILE RIVER

ABYDOS •

The Step Pyramid at Saqqara was the first pyramid built in Egypt.

FAIYUM OASIS

RIVER OF LIFE

The Nile River brought life to the desert lands of Egypt. On its banks, the ancient Egyptians built an extraordinary civilization that lasted for more than 3,000 years. They used the river to transport goods and armies, grew crops on its floodplains, and built great cities on its banks.

Black and red

The ancient Egyptians called the fertile strip near the Nile River *Kemet*, which means "the black land." They associated the color black with life rather than death because it was the color of their soil. Their word for the harsh, desert regions that covered most of Egypt was *Deshret*, which means "the red land."

> CIVILIZATION—*a large, organized group of people who have rules or laws about the way they live or behave*

The temple of Amen was built near the great trading city of Thebes on the east bank of the river.

EASTERN DESERT

VALLEY OF THE KINGS

• **KARNAK**
• **LUXOR**
  (THEBES)

NILE RIVER

VALLEY OF THE QUEENS

• EDFU

For 500 years, tombs were built for pharaohs and powerful nobles in the Valley of the Kings.

• **ASWAN**
• **PHILAE**

WESTERN DESERT

UPPER EGYPT

God of the flood

Hapy was the god of the annual inundation. The Egyptians made offerings to him to make sure that there would be just the right level of flooding for their crops. He was said to be the husband of both the vulture-goddess Nekhbet, protector of Upper Egypt, and the cobra-goddess Wadjyt, protector of Lower Egypt.

THE INUNDATION

Every year, the Nile River flooded, depositing a rich layer of black silt on either side of the banks. This was called the inundation. The crops grown in the enriched soil included barley, emmer wheat, lentils, figs, flax, grapes, pomegranates, and cucumbers. The shadoof (right) that the Egyptians invented to lift water from the river for irrigation is still used today.

Valley transportation

Wooden sailboats have sailed down the protected waters of the Nile for more than 5,000 years. The Nile is the longest river in the world, but through the narrow Nile valley it is never more than 12 mi. (19km) across.

Rameses II's temples at Abu Simbel marked the southern part of the Egyptian empire, where the land bordered Nubia (today's Sudan).

• **ABU SIMBEL**

❯ Even today, 90 percent of Egypt is desert and more than 95 percent of the population live in the Nile valley.

DYNASTIES

The Egyptian historian Manetho of the 200s B.C. divided the kings of Egypt before Alexander the Great into 30 groups called dynasties. This comes from the Greek word *dunamis*, meaning "power." Today, historians place Egyptian civilization into five eras: the Old, Middle, and New Kingdoms; the Late Period; and the Greco-Roman Period, separated from each other other by the First, Second, and Third Intermediate periods.

DYNASTY–a succession of rulers from the same family or line

ALEXANDER THE GREAT
- Ruled 332–323 B.C.
- Ptolemaic Period, Macedonian Kings
Alexander III of Macedonia occupied Egypt and was anointed as pharaoh in Memphis. He restored temples at Luxor and Karnak, and, in 331 B.C., founded Alexandria, which was the capital for 1,000 years.

SHABAQO
- Ruled c. 716–702 B.C.
- Third Intermediate Period, 25th Dynasty
Nubian king Shabaqo reunified a divided Egypt by taking over Lower Egypt. He reinstated the Old Kingdom style of Egyptian art.

AKHENATON
- Ruled 1352–1336 B.C.
- New Kingdom, 18th Dynasty
Amenhotep IV changed his name to Akhenaton and with his queen, Nefertiti, made Aton, the sun, the chief god. He moved the capital from Thebes to Akhetaton.

SENWOSRET III
- Ruled 1872–1842 B.C.
- Middle Kingdom, 12th Dynasty
Senwosret was the great pharaoh of this dynasty. He expanded the empire south into Nubia and east into Palestine. During his reign, there was greater economic prosperity.

NARMER
- Ruled c. 3100 B.C.
- Early Dynastic Period, 1st Dynasty
Many archaeologists think that Narmer, also known as Menes, was the first ruler to unite Egypt, founding the 1st Dynasty.

> Narmer's name, represented by the image of a catfish and chisel, appears written on several carved stone and ivory objects.

CLEOPATRA VII PHILOPATOR
• **Ruled 51–30 B.C.**
• **Ptolemaic Period, Ptolemaic Dynasty**
As Egypt's last pharaoh, Cleopatra held power by forming an alliance first with Julius Caesar and then with Mark Antony. She killed herself when Caesar's heir to Rome, Octavian, defeated the Egyptian forces.

KEY
The pharaohs are displayed in chronological order from 1 to 10.

PSAMTEK I
• **Ruled 664–610 B.C.**
• **Late Period, 26th Dynasty**
The Assyrians occupied Lower Egypt and made Psamtek the area's governor. However, Psamtek freed Egypt from Assyrian control to become ruler of all of Egypt.

CROWNS OF EGYPT

The crown of Upper Egypt was the tall, white *hedjet*. The *deshret*, or red crown, was the crown of Lower Egypt. After Egypt was united by Narmer, pharaohs could wear one or the other, or a combination of the two. From about the 18th Dynasty, pharaohs are often shown wearing the *khepresh*, or blue crown.

combined crown of Upper and Lower Egypt

www.touregypt.net/kings.htm

THUTMOSE III
• **Ruled 1479–1425 B.C.**
• **New Kingdom, 18th Dynasty**
Thutmose ruled as pharaoh for 33 years. He was a superb military leader and tactician and never lost a battle. During his reign, he created the largest empire in the history of ancient Egypt.

RAMESES II
• **Ruled 1279–1213 B.C.**
• **New Kingdom, 19th Dynasty**
This pharaoh reigned for 66 years and was known as Rameses the Great. He built more buildings and statues than any other Egyptian king, including the Great Hypostyle Hall at Karnak.

Triumph in battle
In wall paintings, Rameses II portrayed himself as a fearless military leader. Here, he is shown in his chariot at the Battle of Kadesh, which took place in 1285 B.C. The Egyptian forces were caught in an ambush by the Hittites, but the pharaoh managed to rally his scattered troops, and the battle ended in a truce.

KHUFU
• **Ruled c. 2589–2566 B.C.**
• **Old Kingdom, 4th Dynasty**
This pharaoh's Great Pyramid was one of the seven wonders of the ancient world. The huge size of the pyramid, which took 23 years to build, suggests to historians that Khufu was a tyrant.

PHARAOH GOD

HIERARCHY—government by a system of people ranked one above another

Abu Simbel

Rameses II was worshiped as a living god. He ordered two temples to be carved in sandstone cliffs at Abu Simbel in Nubia. This one has giant carvings of the gods, including Rameses himself.

As ruler of the nation, the pharaoh represented the gods—about 1,500 of them. Both the pharaoh and the ordinary people worshiped these gods and gave them gifts. This ensured that the annual flood took place and that order was upheld. When the pharaoh died, he became protector of the dead and helped their rebirth into a new life.

Gifts to the gods

Discovered in a tomb near Medinet Habu, the extraordinary Great Harris Papyrus, written during the reign of Rameses IV, celebrates Rameses III. It shows the pharaoh making offerings to different groups of gods, including the ones shown below. The three gods on the left are the triad of Memphis, and the next three are the triad of Thebes.

Ptah was a creator god and the god of craftsmen.

Sekhmet was Ptah's wife and the goddess of war.

Nefertem was Ptah and Sekhmet's son and was god of the lotus flower.

Khons was the moon god and son of Amen and Mut.

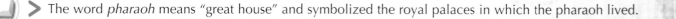

> The word *pharaoh* means "great house" and symbolized the royal palaces in which the pharaoh lived.

Life and death

On Earth, the sun-god in his various guises over the centuries—as Ra, Ra-Harakhty, Amen, and Amen-Ra—was the dominant deity. In the afterlife, the lord of the dead, Osiris, and the god of mummification, the jackal-headed Anubis (left), ruled supreme.

The pharaoh had absolute power over his subjects. However, in practice, he had to rule through a hierarchy of officials. The chief adviser was the vizier, or first minister, followed by other high officials, diplomats, and priests, who helped govern the different parts of Egypt. Scribes were in charge of keeping all records and issuing rules of law.

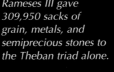

sculpture of an Egyptian scribe

Mut was Amen's wife, daughter of the sun-god Ra, and the mother goddess.

The roles of gods changed over time, and many gods took multiple forms.

Amen was the king of gods and a creator god.

Rameses III gave 309,950 sacks of grain, metals, and semiprecious stones to the Theban triad alone.

PALACE LIFE

MENAGERIE—a collection of wild or exotic animals kept for exhibition

A pharaoh owned several palaces and moved with his household from one to another by royal barge on the Nile River. He also had several wives, one of whom was his chief wife and queen. Egyptian nobles who were in favor would be invited to send their children to court, where they could live and study alongside the royal children.

A royal banquet

Egyptians enjoyed entertaining, and feasts at the palace were elaborate affairs. The pharaoh, his chief wife, and honored guests watched from a raised dais. The remaining guests were seated at tables around the room. They wore garlands and offered flowers to each other as they ate. Servants carried in roast game, fish, vegetables, and fruit, while musicians, dancers, and acrobats entertained them.

Women's tunics could cover one or both shoulders or were worn with shoulder straps.

Men usually wore linen kilts wrapped around their waist.

> A toilet in an Egyptian palace was a low, wooden stool with a hole cut in the seat.

Hieroglyphs were used to decorate the palace pillars.

Artistic license

This picture shows women at a feast. In their hands are bunches of lotus flowers, symbols of rebirth and renewal. On their heads are "perfume cones." These cones are thought to be a device used by the artist to indicate that the women are wearing perfume.

Singers and musicians entertained the palace guests.

JEWELRY AND MAKEUP

Wealthy Egyptians took great care with their appearance for feasts. Both men and women painted heavy black lines in kohl around their eyes, and women rubbed rouge onto their cheeks. Anklets and rings were worn both for their beauty and as a protection from evil.

ornate collar (necklace) from c. 1345 B.C.

gold ring from the 18th Dynasty

Exotic animals

Some pharaohs kept menageries. Many of the animals were given to them by foreign kings, but others were collected when the pharaohs waged war. Rameses II had a pet lion that accompanied him into battle. Thutmose III kept antelope, leopards, ostrich, elephants, rhinoceros, and chickens in his botanical gardens (left).

SCRIBE STORY

A scribe's profession was a respected one in ancient Egypt. The Egyptians valued education, and all the offices of state were open to a scribe because he could read and write in hieroglyphs (picture symbols). Nebamun was "the Scribe and Grain accountant in the Granary of Amen" in Thebes. He died around 1350 B.C. Paintings from his tomb-chapel at Dra Abu el-Naga, opposite Thebes, give us an insight into his life.

Tomb hunter

Paintings on the walls of tombs were laden with symbolism. This wall painting is symbolic in its intention to help Nebamun's rebirth in the afterlife. The Egyptians believed that the world was born out of the marshy waters of chaos. Nebamun's hunting symbolizes his triumph over the chaos in nature, while various symbols of the sun-god ensure Nebamun's rebirth, just like the sun reappearing in the sky every day.

The Painter

These six cups were found by the side of a mummy nicknamed "the Painter" during an excavation at Hawara. They are made of clay from the Nile River. The paintbrush is made from fine palm fibers cut at one end, and there are traces of red pigment on the end of the brush.

> The ancient Egyptians believed that carving a name could help a person live forever.

KEY

1 Nebamun stands on a small papyrus boat. In his left hand is a snake-headed throwing stick, which is being used to hunt waterfowl.

2 Hatshepsut, Nebamun's wife, is dressed in her finest clothes and crowned with lotus flowers and a perfume cone. She is ready for her journey into the afterlife.

3 Nebamun's daughter sits between his legs, picking lotus flowers. Her youth is shown by the lack of clothes and the side lock (single braid of hair).

4 A tawny cat attacks several birds. The gold leaf on the cat's eye suggests that it represents the sun-god Ra, who was reborn every day at dawn.

5 Nebamun's white kilt and overkilt are made of fine linen to represent his wealth. His stomach has small rolls of fat to further indicate his prosperity.

6 A red goose, an animal sacred to Amen, sits on the prow of the boat.

7 On the top of a thick clump of papyrus reeds—marsh plants that were used to make paper for scribes—are three nests containing birds' eggs.

8 The poisonous puffer fish is still found in the Nile River today.

www.britishmuseum.org/explore/galleries/ancient_egypt/room_61_tomb-chapel_nebamun.aspx

Hieroglyphs

Egyptians composed names for everything in their world using picture symbols called hieroglyphs. Here, Rehotep, a prince of the 4th Dynasty, is seated in front of a table on which there are offerings to sustain him in the afterlife. These gifts, including incense, eye paint, wine, and dates, are described in the hieroglyphs.

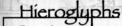

"Egyptian blue" pigment is a human-made copper calcium silicate.

LIFE AT HOME

Egyptian houses were built of bricks made of mud and straw, dried in the sun. In towns, some of the finer houses were two stories high and had bathrooms and toilets. Their walls were plastered and painted with geometric patterns and scenes of plants and birds. During hot weather, many people slept on the roof and sometimes cooked there, too. Household waste was buried in pits or thrown in the river or into the street. Water was drawn from public or private wells.

servants' quarters

servants tending garden

main entrance

PLASTER–a mixture of lime, sand, water, and animal hair that sets and hardens

⊕ HOME FURNISHINGS

Wealthy homes had tiled floors and painted walls. Furniture was minimal and included low stools, chests, tables, and beds. Poor people slept on straw mats, with headrests that had protective images to ward off scorpions and bad dreams.

stone board game with pottery playing pieces

wooden toy cat with movable mouth

Egyptians had large families, and children lived at home until their early teens. Many toys and games have been found in excavations, and children often had birds or dogs as pets. Boys went to school, but girls helped at home.

"I am the most beautiful tree in the garden, And for all times, I shall remain. The beloved and her brother Stroll under my branches, Intoxicated from wines and spirits, Steeped in oil and fragrant essences."

Turin Papyrus
19th Dynasty

Garden houses

In the country, the houses of wealthy Egyptians were set in large, formal gardens surrounded by high walls. At this nobleman's garden house in Akhetaton, trees were grown both for shade and for their fruit, which included dates, figs, pomegranates, and nuts. Vines were planted in straight rows between ponds stocked with fish.

> Baboons were trained to climb fig trees and pick the ripe fruit for their owners.

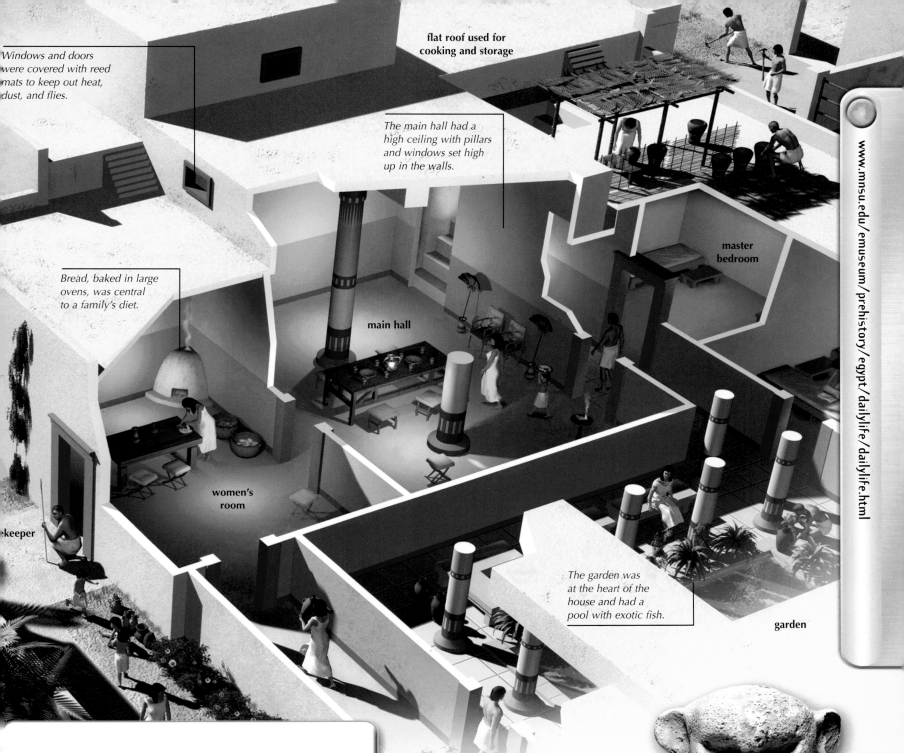

Windows and doors were covered with reed mats to keep out heat, dust, and flies.

flat roof used for cooking and storage

The main hall had a high ceiling with pillars and windows set high up in the walls.

master bedroom

Bread, baked in large ovens, was central to a family's diet.

main hall

women's room

-keeper

The garden was at the heart of the house and had a pool with exotic fish.

garden

In towns

There were set areas used for particular purposes in every house in ancient Egypt, from a basic, mud-brick house to a wealthy home in town (above). The father of the family received guests in a reception area, the mother and children had a private domain, and there was an area for routine tasks, such as food preparation and other everyday chores.

Household gods

There were niches (small hollows) in the house walls where the statues of protective household gods and goddesses were kept. Bes (right), the bearded dwarf-god, frightened away evil spirits, while Bastet, the cat-goddess, warded off infectious diseases. Tawaret, with the head of a hippopotamus, protected women during pregnancy and childbirth.

PYRAMID BUILDER

It took about 20 years and the labor of thousands of men to build one of the seven wonders of the ancient world, the Great Pyramid of Khufu at Giza. Around 5,000 of the workers were full-time employees of the pharaoh, while 20,000 were farm workers, conscripted for a few months of each year when the Nile River flooded the fields.

Workers' graffiti

The workers were organized into crews by their supervisors to develop a competitive team spirit. A crew would comprise about 2,000 men, split into large groups that were then subdivided and given specific tasks. Graffiti shows that the crews of Giza gave themselves names such as "Friends of Khufu" and "Drunkards of Menkaure."

Village of the workers

Specially built villages supported the daily lives of the pyramid workers. The villages were fully functioning, with streets, houses, stores, and a cemetery. The workers and their families were cared for by a dentist and a physician. This is known because archaeologists have found remains of pyramid workers at Giza that show that the Egyptians knew how to realign broken bones.

bakers

fish sellers

physician

> Farm workers had daily rations of ten loaves of bread and a measure of beer.

a Giza team name: "The White Crown of Khufu Is Powerful"

The Great Pyramid is made of about 2.3 million blocks of stone, weighing 2.5 to 15 tons each.

Up to 30,000 workers built the three pyramids of Giza over a period of 80 years.

utchers

granary

blacksmith

copper workshop

⬤ MASTER BUILDERS

The pyramid builders dragged the large blocks of stone for the Great Pyramid 980 ft. (300m) across the desert from the quarry and up ramps to each level as the pyramid grew. They fitted them into place with tools that were not unlike those in use today. Special blocks of white limestone, trimmed to make a smooth surface, covered the outside of the pyramid, and the top was covered in metal to gleam in the sunlight.

saw

chisel

mallet

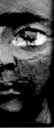

STAIRWAYS TO HEAVEN

The pyramid complex of Giza is on a plateau just south of the modern city of Cairo.

The Egyptians believed that when a pharaoh died, the sun-god Ra strengthened the rays of the sun to allow the ruler to climb to the sky. The shape of a pyramid provided the "stairway to heaven" that was needed. The earliest pyramids were designed in steps. Later, architects competed with one another to build the perfect pyramid.

Menkaure (reigned c. 2532–2504 B.C.) built the third and smallest pyramid, which was 215 ft. (65.5m) tall.

"All the world fears time, but time fears the pyramids."

Arab proverb

Pyramids of Giza

During the 4th Dynasty, three pharaohs contributed to what is the most famous pyramid complex of all. Located at Giza, the largest structure, the Great Pyramid, is the only one of the seven wonders of the ancient world still standing. Near the smallest structure, the pyramid of Menkaure, stand three small pyramids that were built for queens.

> The Great Pyramid was the tallest human-made structure in the world for more than 3,800 years.

Step Pyramid

The first pyramid to be built in Egypt was for the 3rd Dynasty pharaoh King Djoser. Constructed at Saqqara in c. 2650–2575 B.C., it began as a normal mastaba, or tomb, which was a single-story rectangular building with underground rooms for the burial chambers. Later, more mastabas were added on top, until it reached a height of 197 ft. (60m).

The Step Pyramid of Djoser rises in six stages.

Khufu (reigned c. 2589–2566 B.C.), built the Great Pyramid, which was 480 ft. (146.5m) tall.

Khafre (reigned c. 2558–2532 B.C.) built the second-largest pyramid at Giza, which was 471 ft. (143.5m) tall.

Architect to the pharaoh

Imhotep was Djoser's vizier and architect and is credited with being the builder of the Step Pyramid. The Egyptian historian Manetho claims that the architect invented the technique of building in dressed stone. He also writes about Imhotep's list of "instructions" and works on medicine, but nothing has survived of these.

Bent Pyramid

In the first attempt at building a true pyramid with smooth sides, architects began a project at the necropolis of Dahshur, but its angle was too steep. Cracks began to appear, so they changed the angle to make the slope more gradual. This resulted in what is now known as the Bent Pyramid of Sneferu. (Sneferu was a pharaoh of the 4th Dynasty.)

The Bent Pyramid of Sneferu stood 344 ft. (105m) tall.

TOMB RAIDER

Tombs and pyramids in ancient Egypt were often raided for their riches. Tomb raiders were sometimes the men who had built the tombs. If they were caught, they died impaled on wooden stakes. However, it was not uncommon for pharaohs to recycle tomb goods. For example, some of the objects buried with Tutankhamen, including his second inner coffin and the golden bands around his mummy, were taken from the grave goods of Smenkhkare I, who probably ruled for a short time before him.

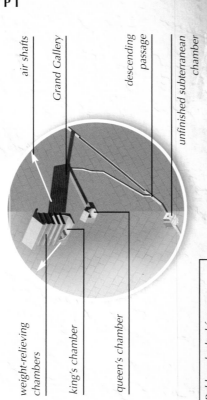

inside the Great Pyramid of Giza

air shafts

Grand Gallery

descending passage

unfinished subterranean chamber

weight-relieving chambers

king's chamber

queen's chamber

Robbers looked for precious metals that could be melted down easily.

Perishable goods, such as expensive oils, spices, wines, and linens, were favorites to steal.

The caliph's men

In A.D. 820, a caliph (Islamic leader) named Abdullah Al-Mamun had his men break into the Great Pyramid of Giza to look for astronomical charts, maps, and treasures. They heated the limestone blocks and doused them in cold vinegar, creating cracks that allowed them to break through. They found only an empty sarcophagus in the king's chamber.

gilded box from the queen's chamber

> SARCOPHAGUS—a stone coffin, often inscribed with texts and decorated with images

THE DIXON RELICS

In 1872, a British engineer, Waynman Dixon, examined the two air shafts leading from the king's chamber and correctly calculated that there were two leading from the queen's chamber. Inside one of these, Dixon found three mysterious objects: a small, bronze hook (below right), a piece of cedarlike wood, and a large, granite ball (below left).

two of the Dixon relics

Handheld torches were used to light the way into the tomb.

The Abbott Papyrus

In about 1100 B.C., there were reports that royal tombs in the Theban necropolis were being raided. This papyrus records the details of an investigation, including the possible corruption of the mayor. It describes the robbery of the tomb of 17th-Dynasty pharaoh Sobekemsaf II and the trial of the robbers after they were beaten to make them confess.

Robot Rover

Inside the Great Pyramid are four air shafts, and there has been a lot of speculation about whether they are really "air shafts" or "passages to heaven" for the deceased pharaoh. These air shafts have been explored using robots, including Rover in 2002.

> Some tombs in the Valley of the Kings were built high up in the cliffside to hide them from robbers.

MUMMIFICATION

When an ancient Egyptian died, it was essential that the body was preserved as a resting place for the spirit. The deceased was taken to the *per nefer*, or "perfect house," where embalmers carried out a mummification process that took up to 70 days. This was intended to ensure the survival of the dead person for all eternity. Statues were also commissioned, which could stand in for the body if it was somehow destroyed.

Animals, such as cats, monkeys, and crocodiles, were mummified for their preservation as pets, sacred animals, or gifts for the gods.

⊖ OPENING OF THE MOUTH

When the mummy was ready to be placed in the coffin, a ritual called the "Opening of the Mouth" was performed by the dead person's son or heir wearing the mask of Anubis, the god of mummification. The ceremony was vital because it meant that the dead person could eat, drink, and move around in the afterlife.

Ay, Tutankhamen's successor, stands before Osiris holding the ceremonial *setep*, or *adze*.

Canopic jars

The liver, intestines, stomach, and lungs were removed during mummification. They were stored for protection in four special containers called canopic jars. The heart was left inside the body so that it could be weighed in the afterlife (see page 24). The stoppers of these jars represent the four sons of Horus, the canopic deities.

In the *ibu*, the place of purification, the embalmers first wash the body with palm wine and then rinse it with water taken from the Nile River.

Here, the stomach is being removed, before being washed, packed with natron, and placed in the canopic jar representing the jackal-headed god Duamutef.

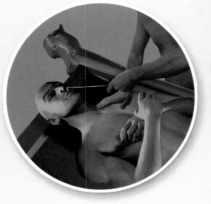

The embalmers use a long hook to smash the brain and then pull it out through the nostrils. Then the whole body is stuffed with and covered in natron.

After 40 days, the body is washed out with Nile water, oiled, and perfumed. The brain cavity is filled with resin or linen and artificial eyes are added.

> A scarab beetle amulet was placed over the heart to ensure it was not separated from the body.

Preparing the dead

The process of mummification changed over time. To begin with, it was available only to kings, but by the New Kingdom (c. 1550–1070 B.C.), it was the practice for anyone who could afford it. The *hery seshta*, or master of secrets, was in charge and took the role of the jackal-god Anubis. Natron salt crystals were used to dehydrate, or dry out, the body. A priest was on hand to recite spells and prayers.

The master of secrets inserts protective amulets between the wrappings while bandaging the body.

The body is stuffed with dry material, such as sawdust and leaves (above), and then oiled again. Finally, it is wrapped in many layers of linen (right) in a process that takes up to 15 days.

www.ancientegypt.co.uk/mummies/story/main.html

THE FINAL JOURNEY

The coffin was carried inside the tomb, together with goods for the deceased to use in the afterlife. Egyptians believed that during their journey through the underworld, they had to win their place in the afterlife. They were judged on their behavior during their lifetime at a ceremony called the "Weighing of the Heart."

The underworld

The Egyptians believed that the path to the underworld was full of dangers, such as snakes and crocodiles. Armed with spells, some written on coffins and others on scrolls of papyrus called "Books of the Dead," the deceased would be able to overcome all the dangers and reach the afterlife.

> "May I walk every day on the banks of the water, may my soul rest on the branches of the trees which I planted, may I refresh myself under the shadow of my sycamore."
>
> **Egyptian tomb description**
>
> *c. 1400 B.C.*

Ancestor gods

When a pharaoh died, many personal items were placed with them in the coffin. Ahhotep I was a powerful queen during the 17th Dynasty. This is her funerary bracelet, made of gold and lapis lazuli. It shows the ancestor souls of the cities of Pe and Nekhen. They are lifting their hands in jubilation to wish the pharaoh "all life and sovereignty."

> Ancient Egyptians provided for the afterlife in a way that reflected their lifestyles on Earth.

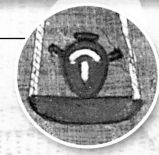

the goddess Ammut

Anubis, god of the dead

Heavy heart

The jackal-headed god Anubis weighed the heart of the deceased against the feather of Maat, the goddess of truth and justice. If the heart was too heavy, it would be eaten by crocodile-headed Ammut, the eater of the dead. The deceased would then die a second death and cease to exist.

Painted coffins

Coffins depicted the person as they would like to look for eternity. They were covered in spells to protect the deceased and preserve his or her spirit. Early coffins were made of wood and were usually rectangular. Later, body-shaped inner coffins (right) made of wood or metal were placed inside outer coffins (far right).

⊙ FUNERARY GOODS

Male and female shabti (figures made in the image of servants) were buried with the dead. They were inscribed with a special formula that enabled the servants to carry out manual work on behalf of the dead person. Shabti were normally made of faience or wood.

painted wooden shabti figures of the Theban priestess Henutmehyt

Arrows fired by the Egyptian marine archers rained on the Sea Peoples.

EGYPT AT WAR

The Egyptian civilization lasted for thousands of years because its rulers were excellent at conquering their enemies and defending their territories. Early kings raided African neighbors, bringing back riches including gold from Nubia. Later pharaohs led their armies into Asia, expanding the Egyptian empire. In 1178 B.C., in a great naval battle near the Nile delta, Egyptian tactics defeated a potentially overwhelming attack by the Sea Peoples, raiders from the eastern Mediterranean.

Delta battle

Rameses III (reigned 1184–1153 B.C.) had already defeated the Sea Peoples on land in southern Palestine. Faced with a formidable fleet carrying thousands of the enemy, he lined the delta's shores with ranks of archers. Then he gave the Egyptian fleet instructions to drive the enemy ships toward the shore, to be targeted by volley after volley of arrows.

Rameses III directed the battle from his chariot.

> The Egyptians believed that they could ward off danger with magic spells and amulets.

MEDICAL SOLUTIONS

The Egyptians had great medical skills that would have been needed in bloody battles. Papyrus manuals show that physicians had a detailed knowledge of anatomy. The Edwin Smith Papyrus describes closing wounds with sutures and stopping bleeding by covering wounds with raw meat. Surgical instruments that have survived include pincers, knives, scissors, scales, and hooks (right).

Egyptian boats forced the enemy toward the land.

Archers fired volleys of arrows from the shore to stop the ships of the Sea Peoples from landing.

SPHINX—a mythical creature, usually with the body of a lion and the head of a human

CITY OF POWER

Ahmose I took back the delta region from the Hyksos (an Asiatic people who invaded the eastern Nile delta), reunified Egypt, and marked the beginning of the New Kingdom (1550–1086 B.C.). His son, Amenhotep I, reestablished Thebes as the capital city, and it remained the seat of power for most of the 18th Dynasty. It was the center of worship for Amen, the king of the gods.

Religious festivals

One of the most important religious holidays during the New Kingdom was the Festival of Mut in Thebes. A statue of the goddess Mut was carried on a bark around the crescent-shaped sacred lake, the "Isheru," that surrounds her temple at Karnak.

Theban triad

Amenhotep III (reigned 1390–1352 B.C.) transformed Thebes by building new temples to worship Amen at Luxor and Karnak. There are three temples inside the Luxor complex near Thebes, sacred to Amen, his wife Mut, and Khons, the moon god and their son.

"The Sphinx is drowsy,
Her wings are furled:
Her ear is heavy,
She broods on the world.
Who'll tell me my secret,
The ages have kept?"

Ralph Waldo Emerson (1803–1882)
American poet, from his poem "The Sphinx" (1841)

> The Great Sphinx of Giza is the largest free-standing sculpture that survives from the ancient world.

Avenue of the Sphinxes

A 2-mi.-long (3-km-long) avenue lined with human-headed sphinxes linked the Luxor temple with the southern end of the Karnak temple complex to the north. Originally there were three avenues of sphinxes built for processions. These statues of lions had human faces or the heads of rams, falcons, or jackals. They symbolized strength, wisdom, and intelligence.

Carved ram

Ram-headed sphinxes lined the avenues of the temple of Rameses II in the Karnak complex. This type of sphinx is a symbol of Amen. Statues of Rameses were placed between the paws. During the annual Opet festival, images of the Theban triad were carried down the avenue on their way to the temple of Mut at Luxor.

The human-headed sphinxes usually had the face of the ruling pharaoh.

◉ COLOSSI OF MEMNON

These enormous seated statues once flanked the gateway in front of the pylon of the mortuary temple of Amenhotep III in the Theban necropolis. The damaged Colossi of Memnon are all that remain of that temple today, but they are almost 60 ft. (18m) high and weigh more than 800 tons.

Each statue was hewed from a single block of stone.

landing
stage

Grain, gathered into
sheaves in the fields,
was used to make
bread and beer.

slave leading cattle to market

TRADE
AND TAXES

MERCHANDISE—goods that are bought and sold by merchants

Wherever there was a town, there was trade. Most
Egyptians were peasant farmers making a living from
agriculture, growing barley for bread and beer, and flax
for linen. They brought their wares to town to exchange
for goods from other traders, such as metalworkers and
potters. As trading relationships developed with other
countries, merchants began to offer exotic imports,
such as spices from Punt, precious stones from
Bactria, and cedar wood from Lebanon.

Beer in pottery jars
could be tasted
before buying.

Taxing the population

Every year, taxes were owed to the pharaoh.
In the case of farmers, taxes were paid either with
produce or labor. Scribes inspected the land, crops,
and animals, calculating how much was due. In this
wall painting, the scribe Nebamun (see pages
12–13) is counting and recording a herd of cattle.

> The domesticated camel was not introduced into Egypt until 500 B.C.

palm-leaf covered shelters

In a workshop, craftsmen bored holes into beads with bow-drills, polished the beads, and assembled jeweled collars.

covering shields goods from the hot sun

Workers cut ripe grapes from overhanging vines and then stomped on them in vats to make wine.

Value systems

Merchants and wealthy people used standard weights of copper, silver, or gold to figure out the worth of goods. For example, a Theban woman named Iritnefer bought a Syrian slave girl for goods deemed to be worth one pound of silver. These goods included a fine robe, two bronze vessels, copper, and a jar of honey.

At the market

Goods were transported by boat down the river and unloaded from the landing area. Local people set up small stalls displaying their vegetables, homemade food, and handcrafted items. Customers bartered for fish, pottery, woven baskets, bread, beer, oil, clothing, and domestic animals, offering items they brought with them in exchange.

RELIGION AND CHANGE

In 1352 B.C., a pharaoh came to power who tried to change everything. Originally named Amenhotep IV, Akhenaton ruled for about 16 years, and from his third year he began to disband the powerful priesthoods and ban the worship of many of the gods, destroying their images. He built the city of Akhetaton (Amarna), where only Aton, the sun disk, and Akhenaton himself were worshiped. He introduced a new philosophy of the natural world that was reflected in compositions such as "The Great Hymn to the Aton" (see below).

Akhenaton

There were many innovations during Akhenaton's reign. His promotion of Aton over Amen was reflected in a revolution in the art of the period. The shape of the pharaoh, as he was depicted, changed, and he was portrayed with elongated features and body. The temples that he built were also different— he worshiped his god in the open air, in temples without roofs.

Family life

Akhenaton's chief wife was named Nefertiti, which means "the beautiful lady is come." She helped her husband establish the cult of Aton. This plaque shows them with three of their six daughters. Akhenaton allowed artists to depict his family life, something that no pharaoh had done before him.

> CULT—a group of people who are bound together by devotion to and worship of a particular person or thing

In 1887, a collection of almost 400 cuneiform documents were discovered at the site of Akhetaton. They are international diplomatic letters, most of them in Akkadian, the Mesopotamian diplomatic language, and were written to the pharaoh. Most date to the reign of Akhenaton.

"At daybreak,
when you arise on the horizon,
When you shine as the Aton by day,
You drive away the darkness
and give your rays.
The Two Lands are in festivity every day,
Awake and standing upon (their) feet,
For you have raised them up.
Washing their bodies,
Taking (their) clothing,
Their arms are (raised) in praise
at your appearance."

from "The Great Hymn to the Aton"

KEY

1 The uraeus represented a sacred serpent and was the emblem of supreme power.

2 A false beard made of gold was worn for public appearances.

3 The *heka* ("ruler"), a scepter like a shepherd's crook, showed that the pharaoh was protector of the people.

4 The shepherd's whip symbolized great power.

○ SUN WORSHIP

The royal family is shown worshiping the Aton sun disk (top right) in this illustration from the pharaoh's tomb. The rays of the sun shine down on them. The king and queen are holding up lotus flowers, and the little princess shakes a sistrum, a percussion instrument used in religious ceremonies.

⟩ The name Amenhotep means "Amen is content," while the name Akhenaton means "of service to Aton."

PHARAOH QUEEN

When Thutmose II died in 1479 B.C., his son by one of his lesser wives became Thutmose III. However, he was only a baby, so Hatshepsut, the main wife, acted as regent. Gradually, Hatshepsut began to take over the reins of power. She held a coronation ceremony, received a new throne name, Maatkare, and was referred to as "he" in official documents. To assert her position, she was depicted in all the ceremonial male attire of a pharaoh.

Senenmut with the crown princess Neferure

Holding power

Hatshepsut became a powerful pharaoh, which was remarkable for a woman in ancient Egypt. She did this with help from court officials, but her most important adviser was her architect, Senenmut. Before she even became pharaoh, Hatshepsut entrusted him with the care of her daughter, Neferure, and he masterminded many monuments, including her mortuary temple.

Carvings and wall paintings show Hatshepsut dressed in the costume of the male monarchs of the New Kingdom—an artificial beard, a kilt, and a crown

> Hatshepsut's royal titles included "daughter of Ra" and "Horus Powerful of Kas."

the central staircase
leading into the temple

the mortuary temple
of Hatshepsut at Deir
el-Bahri, near Thebes

Thutmose III (right)
makes an offering
to the god Horus.

⊖ FEMALE RULERS

Hatshepsut ruled for 23 years, but
she was not the only female pharaoh.
The name of Sobeknefru, in the 12th
Dynasty, is recorded on an official king
list in Memphis. Ahmose-Nefertari
probably acted as coregent for her son
Amenhotep I (reigned 1525–1504 B.C.).
Cleopatra VII, in the A.D. 1st century,
was the last of Egypt's pharaohs.

**statuette of
Ahmose-Nefertari**

Pharaonic duties

Carved on the walls of the Red
Chapel of Hatshepsut at Karnak
are scenes showing the queen
carrying out her pharaonic
duties. Here, wearing royal
regalia, including a false beard,
she runs with the Apis bull
during the Heb Sed festival.

VOYAGE TO PUNT

One spectacular foreign voyage is recorded on the walls of Hatshepsut's temple at Deir el-Bahri. The great expedition to the Land of Punt was not the first journey there, but it is the best recorded. It was a trading mission under the command of a senior official, the Nubian general Nehsi, and involved a journey down the Nile River followed by an extraordinary trek across the Eastern Desert and a long journey across the Red Sea.

The long, slender hulls were taken apart after the ships had sailed down the Nile.

It is thought by some historians that the Land of Punt was today's Eritrea.

MEMPHIS

THEBES

Red Sea

EGYPT

Nile River

LAND OF PUNT

route to Land of Punt

In the Land of Punt

Queen Ati (left) accompanied her husband Parehu, the ruler of Punt, when he greeted the voyagers with offerings. Carvings show the cone-shaped huts perched on stilts in the villages of these people. They also show tropical fauna and flora, including giraffes and palm trees. The Egyptians sometimes called the Land of Punt "god's land" because of the incense produced in the area that was used in the temples.

It has been suggested that Queen Ati suffered from curvature of the spinal column.

Across the desert

The expedition sent by Hatshepsut must have taken many months. There were 210 men traveling in five ships, each 70 ft. (21m) long and rowed by 30 men. The ships had to be dismantled and carried across the Eastern Desert before being reassembled to continue their journey. The 125-mi. (200-km) journey across the Eastern Desert and Red Sea hills took about two months.

> Trade with the Land of Punt continued until the beginning of the 20th Dynasty.

It is recorded that on their return, "the ships were laden with the costly products of the Land of Punt and with its many valuable woods." The treasures included giraffes, baboons, gold, ebony, spices, incense, elephant ivory, frankincense and myrrh trees, throwing sticks, and panther skins.

Giraffes and baboons were brought back for the pharaoh's menagerie (animal collection).

Living myrrh trees with root balls were planted at Deir el-Bahri.

www.touregypt.net/featurestories/punt.htm

Donkeys were used to carry the supplies and goods.

Goods included strings of beads, axes, and weapons for the people of Punt.

The crew carried the heavy, dismantled boats during a long, hot, and dusty journey.

VALLEY OF THE KINGS

In the 18th Dynasty, the pharaohs abandoned pyramid building because these structures were out in the open and difficult to defend against tomb raiders. Instead, they began to build rock-cut tombs in the hills near the west bank of the Nile River, opposite Thebes. The Valley of the Kings, surrounded by easily defended cliffs, remained in use until the end of the 20th Dynasty. At least 63 tombs have been excavated there.

Find of the century

On November 4, 1922, a team led by English Egyptologist Howard Carter uncovered the first of 16 descending steps into the Valley of the Kings. They had discovered the entrance to the tomb of the boy pharaoh Tutankhamen (reigned 1336–1327 B.C.), containing many of the possessions originally placed there for the pharaoh to use in the afterlife.

The red sandstone sarcophagus of Tutankhamen contained three coffins nesting inside one another.

burial chamber

Ransacked by robbers, the annex held empty containers and artifacts.

annex

antechamber

> SHRINE—*a container for the statue of a god or the remains of a dead person*

treasury

One of the four miniature gold coffins, decorated with colored glass and semiprecious stones, that contained viscera (internal body organs)

Boats, gilded figures, and a superb canopic chest were among the treasures found here.

Historic discovery

Howard Carter (kneeling) peers at Tutankhamen's sarcophagus through the open doors of the four gilded shrines nesting inside one another in the burial chamber. The tomb had been broken in to by raiders on at least two occasions but was resealed by the necropolis guards.

staircase

passage

the astronomical ceiling in the crypt

> The fingerprints of one of the men who robbed Tutankhamen's tomb are still visible inside a jar of ointment.

This room's contents included dismantled chariots, food, animal-shaped beds, thrones, jewelry, and sandals.

PAINTED LEGACY

One of the largest tombs in the Valley of the Kings is that of Seti I (reigned 1294–1279 B.C.). It is more than 394 ft. (120m) long, and dug deep into a hillside. Discovered in 1817 by an Italian explorer, Giovanni Battista Belzoni, it has remarkable wall paintings. The ceiling in the crypt is vaulted and painted with stars.

TEMPLES OF KARNAK

The temples were covered in brightly colored pictures and hieroglyphs.

Construction at Karnak began in the 20th century B.C. during the Middle Kingdom and continued until Ptolemaic times. The largest temple complex in Egypt had the input of 30 pharaohs, and there is no structure more magnificent than the Great Temple of Amen, enlarged and rebuilt over 2,000 years. The other main buildings of Karnak include temples to Montu and Ptah, as well as to Mut, Amen's wife, and Khons, their son.

Dog-faced baboons

On one of the small buildings near the sacred lake of the temple of Amen are carvings of dog-faced baboons. They face east and are described as "the eastern souls who worship Ra." Baboons were also said to guard the first gate of the underworld.

Great Temple of Amen

The temple layout followed a typical pattern. Its monumental first pylon (gateway) led to an open court. A second pylon then opened into the Great Hypostyle Hall, a roofed structure with many columns. Beyond that there were more pylons and smaller rooms and, finally, the innermost sanctuary, where a shrine contained the cult image of Amen.

> The Great Hypostyle Hall is the largest room of any religious building in the world.

www.eyelid.co.uk/Karnak1.htm

Great Hypostyle Hall

In the magnificent Great Hypostyle Hall were 134 papyrus-shaped columns arranged in 16 rows. The ceiling was 82 ft. (25m) high and would have been decorated with stars or a scene showing the passage of the sun-god through the sky. Three pharaohs contributed to its construction— Rameses I, Seti I, and Rameses II.

Different pharaohs added pylons to the temple, so there are ten gateways.

◉ WORSHIP

The inner sanctum of the temple was closed to everyone except priests and the pharaoh. Senior priests attended daily to the needs of the particular god by looking after his or her cult image and making offerings to it. During festivals, the image of the god would have been sailed across the sacred lake of the temple on a golden barge.

Rameses II built more temples than any other pharaoh.

END OF A CIVILIZATION

From the 600s B.C., Egypt was invaded by foreign powers. These included the Assyrians, the Persians, and the Macedonian Greeks led by Alexander the Great. In 309 B.C., Alexander's general, Ptolemy, founded a Greek-speaking dynasty that ruled from Alexandria. Egypt retained its identity until the death of the last Greek ruler, Cleopatra, in 30 B.C., when Egypt became part of the Roman Empire.

Alexander the Great

In 332 B.C., 24-year-old Alexander III of Macedon marched into Egypt. He was welcomed as a liberator because the Egyptians had suffered exploitation and taxes during the occupation by the Persians, who also did not respect their traditions. Alexander was anointed pharaoh in Memphis on November 14, but he left Egypt only six months after he had arrived.

Apis bull

Alexander was acutely aware of the need to show respect for Egyptian customs. In Upper Egypt, he found it easy to think of Amen as a form of the chief Greek god, Zeus. In Lower Egypt, he offered sacrifices to the Apis bull, the cult animal of the creator god Ptah.

> Cleopatra spoke several languages and was the only Ptolemaic pharaoh who learned Egyptian.

Alexandria

During his stay in Egypt, Alexander founded the city of Alexandria on the Mediterranean coast, but he did not live to see it completed. The city later became the capital of Egypt under the Ptolemaic kings. It was famous for its lighthouse at Pharos (right) and its library, which was the largest in the ancient world.

Cultural identity

This is the mummy case of a man named Artemidorus, who died in about A.D. 100–120 in Hawara, Egypt. It is a good example of the merging of different cultures. The portrait is in the Roman style, his Greek personal name is inscribed on it, and the mummy has been preserved in the traditional Egyptian way.

⊖ FINAL PHARAOH

Cleopatra VII Philopator (reigned 51–30 B.C.) originally shared power with her brothers, Ptolemy XIII and Ptolemy XIV. She became sole ruler with the support of Julius Caesar and, later, Caesar's general Mark Antony. She committed suicide after losing to the Romans at the Battle of Actium.

Cleopatra killed herself with the bite of an asp.

www.bbc.co.uk/history/historic_figures/alexander_the_great.shtml

Alexander's general reigned as Ptolemy (305–282 B.C.). He consolidated Greek rule in Egypt and founded the legendary library of Alexandria.

GLOSSARY

amulet

A charm believed to offer magical protection against evil and danger.

archaeologist

A scientist who studies human history through the excavation and analysis of objects and artifacts.

architect

Someone who designs and supervises the construction of buildings.

artifact

A tool, weapon, or decorative object, often found at an archaeological site, that can help archaeologists understand more about the society that produced it.

bark

A sailing ship or boat.

barter

To bargain for and exchange goods.

Books of the Dead

Spells written on papyrus and placed in tombs from the New Kingdom until the Greco-Roman period.

canopic jar

A special container for storing one of the internal organs of a deceased person.

culture

A set of customs, beliefs, and values belonging to a particular time, place, or group of people.

cuneiform

Mesopotamian script written on clay tablets using wedge-shaped strokes.

decree

An order that has the force of law.

delta

A triangular area of land at the mouth of a large river where it divides into several smaller streams and flows into the sea.

dressed stone

Stone that has been shaped with a hammer and chisel.

empire

A group of different countries, lands, or peoples under the control of one ruler.

excavation

The site of a dig to uncover or unearth artifacts or remains from the past.

faience

Glazed pottery made by baking quartz sand with other minerals.

flax

A flowering plant cultivated for its fibers, which are spun into linen cloth.

graffiti

Pictures or writing drawn or scratched onto a wall or other surface.

hieroglyph

A symbol or small picture representing a word, sound, or idea, used as the basis for ancient Egyptian writing.

inundation

The annual flooding of the Nile River during the summer.

irrigation

The process of bringing a flow of water to dry farmland, often by canals or diverted streams.

kohl

A black powder used as a cosmetic to darken the rims of the eyelids.

mastaba

A type of Early Dynastic and Old Kingdom tomb that was rectangular and had a flat roof.

mercenary

A professional soldier hired to fight.

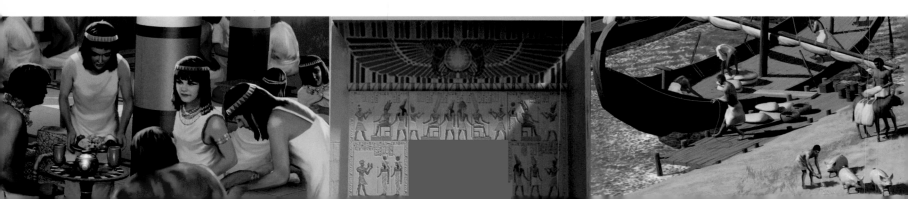

mummification

The process of embalming and drying a body to prepare it for preservation and burial.

natron

A moisture-absorbing salt used to dry a corpse during mummification.

Nubia

A country to the south of Egypt in the area of modern-day Sudan.

papyrus

A tall, riverside reed, the stem of which was used to make boats, rope, baskets, and paperlike sheets for writing.

pharaoh

The title, meaning "great house," given to the rulers of ancient Egypt.

Ptolemaic

Relating to the dynastic house of the Ptolemies and their rule (305–30 B.C.), and the descendants of Alexander the Great's general, Ptolemy.

pylon

The grand entrance to a temple, consisting of tall towers flanking a doorway.

regalia

A collection of objects symbolizing power or rank.

resin

A sticky substance that oozes from pine trees.

sacrifice

The act of offering something to a god, especially the ritual slaughter of an animal or a human being.

scarab

A representation of a dung beetle, used by the ancient Egyptians as a symbol, seal, hieroglyph, or amulet.

shabti

Figures buried with important people so that they could perform manual tasks as servants to the dead in the afterlife.

silicate

Any of many compounds containing silicon, oxygen, and one or more metals.

suture

The joining of a wound by stitches or a similar method.

symbolism

The practice of representing things with symbols or giving them a special meaning or character.

throwing stick

A wooden hunting tool, similar to a boomerang, used to injure or kill prey.

tyrant

A ruler who uses power negatively, governing the nation with cruelty and injustice.

uraeus

The figure of a rearing cobra, worn by pharaohs on the forehead as an emblem of supreme power.

vizier

The highest official in the Egyptian government.

INDEX

ancient Egyptian hieroglyphs

INVESTIGATE

Discover how archaeologists and other experts have unearthed the history of this extraordinary civilization by checking out museums, art galleries, books, and websites.

Museums and art galleries

Visit the many museums, art galleries, and special exhibitions displaying objects that archaeologists have discovered, as well as depictions of life in ancient Egypt.

📖 *The Usborne Encyclopedia of Ancient Egypt* by Gill Harvey and Struan Reid (Usborne)

✦ The Metropolitan Museum of Art, 1000 Fifth Avenue at 82nd Street, New York, NY 10028

🔵 www.egyptianmuseum.org

scarab beetle, the ancient Egyptian symbol for rebirth

elaborately patterned glass jar from the 18th Dynasty

Books and magazines

Find out facts for yourself by reading information books and specialist magazines about ancient Egypt.

📖 *Voyages: Ancient Egypt* by Simon Adams (Kingfisher)

✦ Visit your local library to discover a wide range of books about ancient Egypt.

🔵 http://ngm.nationalgeographic.com/ngm/egypt/egyptfile.html

Great Sphinx of Giza, built by Khafre

people have sailed down the Nile River for thousands of years

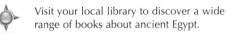

Television and movies

Follow documentaries and dramas about the personalities who ruled ancient Egypt and watch movies that portray life along the banks of the Nile.

📖 *Unlocking the Great Pyramid* by Bob Brier (National Geographic DVD)

✦ The History Channel: Ancient Egypt

🔵 www.ancientnile.co.uk/films.php